Brighter Grammar 4

An English Grammar with Exercises
New edition

C E Eckersley
Margaret Macaulay
Revised by D K Swan

Longman

Addison Wesley Longman Limited
Edinburgh Gate, Harlow
Essex CM20 2JE, England
and Associated Companies throughout the world.

First published 1953
This edition 1987
Fourteenth impression 1998

ISBN 0 – 582 – 55898 – 0

Set in 10/12pt Linotron Times
Produced through Longman Malaysia, ACM

Illustrated by David Mostyn

Contents

(Each lesson is followed by exercises)

Contents

(Each unit is followed by exercises)

Adjective clauses 1

Revision. A **dependent clause** is a sentence that does not make complete sense by itself. It depends on another clause for its full meaning. The chief clause in a sentence (usually the one on which the dependent clauses depend) is called the **main clause**. A **main clause** and one or more **dependent clauses** together make a **complex sentence**.

An **adjective clause** does the work of an **adjective**: it qualifies a **noun**. The adjective clause must go as near as possible to the noun it qualifies.

A **relative pronoun** does the work of both a **pronoun** and a **conjunction**. It stands instead of a **noun** and joins an **adjective clause** to another **clause** in a **complex sentence**.

If you are not quite sure about **adjective clauses** and **relative pronouns** read again Book 3, Lessons 17 and 18, because we are now going to have some rather more difficult examples of their use.

Here are some pairs of **simple sentences**. We will make them into **complex sentences** by using **relative pronouns**.

1 (a) I liked the song.   (b) Margaret sang it.
2 (a) Here are the pictures.   (b) The artist painted them.
3 (a) Sing the song.   (b) You sang it last night.
4 (a) Look at the big tree.   (b) The woodcutter cut it
                                      down yesterday.

5 (a) That is the man.   (b) I met him on Friday.
6 (a) I know that girl.   (b) You spoke to her.

7 (a) Here is the man.   (b) I was helped by him.
8 (a) This is the train.   (b) I came by it.

Now here are those sentences joined together to make
complex sentences. In all these sentences, you can leave out
the relative pronoun *that*.

1 I liked the song (that) Margaret sang.
2 Here are the pictures (that) the artist painted.
3 Sing the song (that) you sang last night.
4 Look at the big tree (that) the woodcutter cut down
   yesterday.
5 That is the man (that) I met on Friday.
6 (i) I know the girl (that) you spoke to.
    OR
   (ii) I know the girl to whom you spoke.
7 (i) Here is the man (that) I was helped by.
    OR
   (ii) Here is the man by whom I was helped.
8 (i) This is the train (that) I came by.
    OR
   (ii) This is the train by which I came.

Now look for a moment at those **pronouns** in the sentences
(b), the pronouns *it, them, it, it, him, her, him, it*.

They are all **objective**, either because they are **objects** of
transitive verbs, or (numbers 6, 7 and 8) because they are
governed by **prepositions**. We replaced them by **relative
pronouns** when we made the **complex sentences**. Those
relative pronouns are objective too, for the same reason.

There is no difference in form between **subjective** *that* and
objective *that* as a **relative pronoun**.

There is an **objective** form *whom* for people. As the object of
a verb, you can leave it out of sentences like:
    That is the man whom I met on Friday.

If you don't leave it out, you are being formal. So we have three degrees of formality:

That's the man I met on Friday. (informal, natural)

That's the man that I met on Friday. (less informal, fairly natural)

That is the man whom I met on Friday. (formal, rather unnatural)

Sentences 6(ii), 7(ii) and 8(ii) are very formal indeed. When there is a **preposition** (*to, by*, etc.) before the **relative pronoun**,

a you can't use *that*;

b you can't leave out the **pronoun**;

c you use *whom* for people, *which* for animals, things and ideas.

You should aim to understand such sentences, but you will hardly ever use them yourself. They are very formal.

Lesson One

Restrictive and non-restrictive adjective clauses

Now we must look at **adjective clauses** of a rather different
kind. An **adjective**, you remember, usually limits the
meaning of a **noun** (Book 1, Lesson 6), and the **adjective
clauses** we have looked at so far also limit the meanings of
the nouns they qualify.

I liked the song. – Any song? No.
Only the song *that Margaret sang*.
Here are the pictures. – Any pictures? No.
Only the pictures *that the artist painted*.

The meaning of the **nouns** is **restricted** by the **adjective
clauses**.

But sometimes a **noun** in the **main clause** is not restricted in
this way:

This is Tom Bates, whom you met on Friday. He lives in
Golders Green, which is a suburb of London.

The meaning of *Tom Bates* is not restricted by the clause
whom you met on Friday: there is only one Tom Bates. We
suppose that there is only one Golders Green, so the
adjective clause doesn't restrict the meaning. The clauses
whom you met on Friday and *which is a suburb of London*
are **non-restrictive adjective clauses**.

Now look at this example:

He lives beside the River Thames, which flows through
London.

Notice the comma (,) that separates the **non-restrictive
adjective clause** from the **noun** it qualifies, the *River Thames*.
We know which River Thames we mean, and we don't need
the clause to distinguish it from any other. But there are
other rivers called 'Thames'.

There is a Thames River *which flows through New London
in Connecticut, U.S.A.*
There is a Thames River *which flows through London,
Ontario, Canada.*

The **adjective clauses** in those two sentences *do* restrict the meaning of *Thames River*. Notice that there is no comma separating the **restrictive adjective clause** from the noun (*Thames River*) it qualifies.

Compare these sentences. The 'A' sentences have **restrictive adjective clauses** limiting (restricting) the meaning of the **noun**. The 'B' sentences have **non-restrictive adjective clauses**: we already know the full meaning of the **noun**, and the sentence makes complete sense without the **adjective clause**.

A	B
Restrictive	*Non-restrictive*
1 Jane is the girl *who is going to be my wife*.	We are waiting for Jane, *who is going to be Jack's wife*.
2 I want you to meet the girl *whom/that I'm going to marry*.	He wanted them to meet Jane, *whom he intended to marry*.
3 He even loves the old bicycle *which* (or *that*) *brings Jane to him*.	Jane was on her old bicycle, *which was bright red*.
4 That's the bicycle *that Jane rides*.	That is Jane's old bicycle, *which she has painted red*.

Notice these things:
1 The comma after the **main clause** in the 'B' sentences. When we are speaking, our voice falls to a lower tone before the comma: ⌐
    We are waiting for Jane, who . . .
    Jane was on her old bicycle. which . . .
  That is because the main clause is a complete statement.
2 We can – and when we are speaking we usually do – leave out the **objective relative pronoun** in the 'A' sentences with **restrictive adjective clauses**.
3 We never leave out the **relative pronoun** in 'B' sentences with **non-restrictive adjective clauses**.

Here is a table of **relative pronouns**. If the word is in square brackets [   ], we usually leave it out unless we are being formal.

	Restrictive		*Non-restrictive*	
	People	*Not people*	*People*	*Not people*
Subjective	who that	which that	who	which
Objective	[whom] [that]	[which] [that]	whom	which

Exercises

A Join each of these pairs of **simple sentences** to make one **complex sentence** with a **restrictive adjective clause**. If you can leave out the **relative pronoun**, put it in square brackets [   ].

Example: That is the bicycle. Jane rides it.
Answer: That is the bicycle [that] Jane rides.

1 We liked the girl. Jack is going to marry her.
2 That is the old bicycle. She rides it.
3 Jack loves a girl. She rides a red bicycle.
4 We know some students. They are learning English grammar.
5 There is the old bicycle. It brings Jane to our house.
6 I am looking for the book. I was reading it last night.
7 Has Ali taken the book? I left it on this table.
8 Did you see a young man? He was eating a sandwich.
9 Is it the young man? We saw him on Saturday.
10 Where is the man? Jane is going to marry him.

B Look at these sentences, pick out the **adjective clause**, and say whether it is **restrictive** (R) or **non-restrictive** (NR).

Example: He is writing to his mother, who wrote to him last
            week.
Answer: who wrote to him last week (NR).

1   I am writing to those nice people we met on holiday.
2   I am writing to Mr and Mrs Lee, who were in Spain with
    us.
3   They looked in the guide book, which had a good map of
    the town.
4   You didn't read the book he sent you.
5   He sent you a book you didn't want.
6   Velma went to Spain with Joanna, who speaks Spanish
    well.
7   Velma went to Spain with a friend who spoke Spanish.
8   Which is the clause that qualifies the noun?
9   We wanted to visit Rome, which is the capital city of
    Italy.
10 Do you remember Madame Duval, whom you met in
    Paris?

C Write down 10 **adjective clauses** in this description and say
whether they are **restrictive** or **non-restrictive**. The first one
is *that was very fine* (R).

Madame Duval had a house that was very fine. It was in a
street which had a lot of fine houses in it, and Madame
Duval knew all the people who lived there. She was very
fond of her only daughter, who lived with her. But she was
afraid of her eldest son, who lived in New York. And she
never saw her son who lived in China or her son who
worked in Port of Spain.
    Madame Duval carefully cleaned the car her daughter
drove, but she couldn't drive herself. She didn't often travel
in the buses that came along the next street or in the taxis
she saw outside her door.

Lesson Two

Adjective clauses 2

End prepositions

JOHN: In Lesson 1 there were three examples:

6(ii) I know the girl *to whom* you spoke.

7(ii) Here is the man *by whom* I was helped.

8(ii) This is the train *by which* I came.

The advice about these on page 7 is that we must aim to understand them but they are very formal and we will hardly ever use them. May I ask two questions? First, why must we understand them? Second, what do we use instead?

TEACHER: First, you must understand them because you will read them in official notices and papers and in some books. You will also hear them in formal speeches and from some people who can't talk simply.

Official: 'The statement also shows the date *by which the payment must reach us*.'

In formal reading: 'There is another fairly common construction *in which we make an addition to a remark*.'

In speeches: 'Ladies and Gentlemen, I am proud to represent the association *for which I speak*.'

Second, instead of beginning the **adjective clause** with a **preposition**, you can end it with the **preposition**:

6(i) I know the girl (that) you spoke to.

7(i) Here is the man (that) I was helped by.

8(i) This is the train (that) I came by.

Some **prepositions** don't easily go at the end of the sentence like that, especially time prepositions like *during*, *before*, and *after*. In most cases you can get round the problem by avoiding the **adjective clause** construction:

Not usual: ~~That was the programme that I fell asleep during.~~

Very formal: That was the programme *during which I fell asleep.*

Simple sentences: Yes, I remember that programme. *I fell asleep during it.*

You remember that the **adjective clause** sometimes divides the **main clause** (Book 3, Lesson 17). What happens then, Richard?

RICHARD: The **adjective clause** goes as near as possible to the **noun** it qualifies.

TEACHER: Well done, Richard. Here are some examples of 'divided' **complex sentences** with **relative pronouns** that are **objective**:

Simple sentences	*Complex sentences*
1 The boy is Richard Brown. I asked him about divided sentences.	The boy (*that/whom*) *I asked about divided sentences* is Richard Brown.
2 The girl is Grace Sangster. You spoke to her.	The girl (*that/whom*) *you spoke to* is Grace Sangster.
3 The train was ten minutes late. I came by it.	The train (*that/which*) *I came by* was ten minutes late.

Numbers 2 and 3 could be:

The girl to whom you spoke is Grace Sangster.

The train by which I came was ten minutes late.

but those sentences would be too formal for conversation.

Whose

Here are some more pairs of **simple** sentences which we will turn into **complex** ones by using a relative pronoun:

(a) I saw the girl.	(b) Her sheep were lost.
(a) This is the boy.	(b) Tom borrowed his bicycle.
(a) We read about the men.	(b) Their deeds thrilled the world.
(a) The boy has gone to Hong Kong.	(b) His father came to see you.

You will notice that in the (b) sentences we have the determiners *her, his, their, his*. These **determiners** are **possessive adjectives**. They qualify the nouns *sheep, bicycle, deeds, father*.

We can make the pairs of **simple sentences** above into **complex sentences**, by using *whose*, the **possessive** form of the relative pronoun *who*.

I saw the girl *whose* sheep were lost.

This is the boy *whose* bicycle Tom borrowed.

We read about the men *whose* deeds thrilled the world.

The boy *whose* father came to see you has gone to Hong Kong.

Note that the relative pronoun *whose* must go next to the **noun** it qualifies.

WAYNE: The adjective clauses in those examples are all **restrictive**. What about **non-restrictive** adjective clauses dividing main clauses?

TEACHER: Good question, Wayne. We use *whose* in the same way, but I will write some examples on the board. I want you to see the commas that mark off the **non-restrictive** clauses.

Joan Denny, whose father is a teacher, has a lot of books.

That black cat, whose owner you have just seen, lives next door.

This book, whose author is an Egyptian, is all about Egypt.

Lesson Two

Exercises

A Take out the relative pronouns *whom* or *which* and
rewrite the sentences putting the **prepositions** in their proper
places. The sentences you write will be less formal.

Example: Who owns the house in front of which we are
standing?
Answer: Who owns the house we are standing in front of?

1 This is the train by which I came.
2 Do you know the boy to whom I am referring?
3 There is the man to whom I wrote the letter.
4 Who is the boy to whom you were talking?
5 This is the tree about which I told you.
6 The children to whom you spoke are learning grammar.
7 The man from whom I got the information is the pilot.
8 The chair on which he sat had just been painted.
9 The people with whom I live are very pleasant.
10 That is the box out of which he took the money.

B Join each of the following pairs of **simple sentences** into
one **complex sentence** by using the relative pronoun *whose*.
The answers to those marked * will be 'divided' complex
sentences.

1 (a) There is the man.   (b) His dog bit me.
* 2 (a) The pilot has flown   (b) I went in his plane.
      10,000 miles.
3 (a) We travelled with a   (b) His plane had flown
      pilot.   round the world.
* 4 (a) The man works at a   (b) His dog bit me.
      garage.
5 (a) I am looking for a   (b) Its title is 'Brighter
      book.   Grammar'.

These are the same, but the **adjective clause** will be **non-restrictive**. Don't forget the commas. The answers to those marked * will be 'divided' complex sentences.

6	(a) He introduced us to Mrs Smith.	(b)	Her house is next to ours.
7	(a) I like their house.	(b)	Its garden is very beautiful.
* 8	(a) This book is a very useful one.	(b)	Its title is 'Brighter Grammar'.
* 9	(a) Carmen has invited us to tea.	(b)	Her mother makes very good cakes.
*10	(a) The pilots are all very good.	(b)	Their training course is a long one.

C Copy these sentences. Draw a box round each **relative pronoun** and draw an arrow pointing to the **noun** that the **adjective clause** qualifies. If there is no **relative pronoun** put a mark like this ∧ .

Examples: There is the man to ⬛ whom ⬛ I wrote the letter.

I like the song ∧ Margaret sang.

1 The burglar who stole the jewels has been caught.
2 I didn't like the people we met.
3 The boy whose dog was lost was very unhappy.
4 I can't find the book I've just bought.
5 There is the girl whose song you liked.
6 The girl who sang the song was Joyce.
7 The picture which hung on the wall has fallen down.
8 I didn't read the book he sent me.
9 Jim MacDonald, whose mother lives in Edinburgh, writes a letter to her every week.
10 John Lennon and Paul McCartney, who wrote the music for 'A Hard Day's Night', were two of the Beatles.

Lesson Three

Adverb clauses

Revision. An **adverb clause** does the work of an **adverb**. It usually modifies a **verb**.

Clauses that tell 'how' an action is done are **adverb clauses of manner**; those that tell 'when' an action is done are **adverb clauses of time**; those that tell 'where' an action happens are **adverb clauses of place**.

You have had, so far, three kinds of **adverb clause: manner**, **time** and **place**. But there are some other kinds of **adverb clause** that you ought to know. They all tell something about the action or fact named by the **verb** in the **main clause**. And from what they tell us we decide what kind of **adverb clause** they are.

Reason

Look at these sentences:
 The thief ran away *because he saw the policeman*.
 Louis passed his examination *because he worked hard*.
 Because he hadn't worked hard, Richard didn't pass his examination.
Why did the thief run away? Why did Louis pass his examination? Why didn't Richard pass? What was the *reason* for his failure?

Clauses that tell 'why' something happened are adverb clauses of reason.

Condition

The sentences in the next group are rather different.

Richard will learn grammar *if he works hard*.

If the rain stops, I'll go for a walk.

We'll help you *if you need help*.

I can't read it *unless you write clearly*.

These sentences tell us *on what condition* Richard will learn grammar, *on what condition* I will go for a walk, *on what condition* we will help, and *on what condition* I can read something.

Clauses that express the condition on which an action was done, is done, or will be done, are called adverb clauses of condition.

Concession

There is another kind of **adverb clause** that I think you ought to know. You will meet sentences like this:

Although Richard tried harder last term, his work is still not good enough.

The line of thought in the sentence is: 'I agree that Richard tried harder' or 'I'll grant you that Richard tried harder' or 'I'll concede the fact that Richard tried harder, but in spite of all that, his work is still not good enough.'

So, because sentences like this 'concede' something, they are called **adverb clauses of concession**. Here are some further examples:

Though there was no hope of winning, the team played their hardest to the very end of the game.

He is a very active man *though he is over eighty*.

Although Richard got up early, he was late in arriving at school.

Although the work looks difficult, it is really quite simple.

19

Lesson Three

Though I was telling him the truth, he still didn't believe me.

Adverb clauses of concession 'concede' or 'grant' a fact. The action or situation named by the verb in the main clause happens in spite of that fact.

Exercise

Analyse the following **complex sentences** containing a **main clause** and an **adverb clause**. Say what kind of adverb clause it is and what function it performs. (The function of a clause means the work it is doing.) Number 1 is done for you.

Principal clause	Adverb clause	Kind	Function
I need a hammer and nails	because I am going to repair the shed	Reason	Modifies the verb 'need'

1 I need a hammer and nails because I am going to repair the shed.
2 We couldn't play the match because the fog was too thick.

3 We shall come and see you if we have a holiday.
4 Although it was rather foggy, we played the match.
5 We shall play the match, even though it is rather foggy.
6 We had to cancel the match because it was so foggy.
7 Russ Conway played the piano well though he couldn't use all his fingers.
8 I will tell you the secret if you won't tell it to anyone else.
9 If you will tell me the secret, I won't tell it to anyone else.
10 They went swimming although the sea was very rough.
11 If I get all these sentences right, I'll have done well.
12 Mrs Brown locked the cupboard because she didn't want Richard to take the cakes.

Clauses 1

A conversation between Miss Macaulay (teacher), Mary, Francine, Joanna, Jane and Elizabeth

MARY: Miss Macaulay, do you ever have two **dependent clauses** in a sentence? All the sentences you have given us so far have had one **main clause** and one **dependent clause** – an **adjective clause** or an **adverb clause** or a **noun clause**.

TEACHER: Well, let us examine your question, Mary. Here is a very simple sentence:

The boy said something.

Now, Francine, will you give us a **noun clause** instead of *something*.

FRANCINE: 'The boy said *that he was hungry*.' Is that right?

TEACHER: That is quite a good **noun clause**. As you give me additions I'll write them on the blackboard. *The boy said* is the **main clause**; *that he was hungry* is a **noun clause**, object of *said*.

Now, Mary, can you add an **adjective clause**? First of all, what do adjective clauses do?

MARY: They do the work of an **adjective**, they qualify a **noun**.

TEACHER: Good. Well, there is only one noun (*boy*) in that sentence so we need an adjective clause to qualify the noun *boy*.

MARY: Well, if he was hungry, he might be crying, so I will add:

The boy, *who was crying*, said that he was hungry.

TEACHER: Well done, Mary. You have given us a **non-restrictive adjective clause**. But we haven't got an **adverb clause** yet, have we? Joanna, could you help us with an adverb clause?

JOANNA: Well, I think I could say *how* he was crying; and clauses that tell *how* something is done are **adverb clauses of manner**. So I will say:

The boy, who was crying *as if his heart would break*, said that he was hungry.

TEACHER: You have helped us a lot, Joanna. Now could we add any more clauses, Jane?

JANE: I think I could add an **adverb clause of time**. Would this be right?

The boy, who was crying as if his heart would break, said, *when I spoke to him*, that he was hungry.

TEACHER: That was good work, Jane. But I think we could add still one more clause. Will you try, Elizabeth?

ELIZABETH: I can add an **adverb clause of reason**.

The boy, who was crying as if his heart would break, said, when I spoke to him, that he was hungry *because he had had no food for two days*.

TEACHER: Well, Mary, I think that has answered your question.

MARY: Oh yes, Miss Macaulay, I see now that a **complex sentence** contains one **main clause** and one or more **dependent clauses**.

TEACHER: Yes, There are six clauses there. You can tell at once how many **clauses** there are in a **complex sentence** by noting how many **finite verbs** there are (see Book 2,

Lesson 20). Each **finite verb** represents a **clause**. If there are three finite verbs there will be three clauses. If there are ten finite verbs there will be ten clauses and so on.

Now let us take to pieces (or *analyse*) the sentence we have just put together. We will set it down like this.

Clause	Kind
The boy . . .	Part of main clause
. . . who was crying . . .	Adjective clause qualifying *boy*
. . . as if his heart would break . . .	Adverb clause (*manner*) modifying *was crying*
. . . said . . .	Part of main clause
. . . when I asked him . . .	Adverb clause (*time*) modifying *said*
. . . that he was hungry . . .	Noun clause, object of *said*
. . . because he had had no food for two days.	Adverb clause (*reason*) modifying *was (hungry)*

I think I want to say one more thing. We have analysed a 6-clause sentence, but don't think that you need to make long complex sentences in your speaking or writing. It isn't necessary, and it often causes you to make mistakes.

Exercise

Analyse these **complex sentences** in the same style as above.

1 The pirates, who had hidden the treasure on the island, went back again because they thought that they could now remove it with safety.
2 Richard, though he had not previously answered any questions when the teacher asked him, now said that he

knew the answer to this one because it was in the lesson
that he had just read.

3 When the teacher asked what part of speech a word was,
Gloria said, 'I can tell you the answer if you will give me a
sentence the word is used in.'

Clauses 2

A conversation between the teacher, Richard, George, Lloyd, John and Harry

RICHARD: I have discovered an easy way of telling whether a clause is one of time or place and so on. This is my method: if it begins with *when* (a 'time' word) it is a time clause; if it begins with *where* (a 'place' word) it's a place clause; if it begins with *if* it's an adverb clause of condition; and if it begins with *who* it's an adjective clause.

TEACHER: Richard, with most things in life there is a right way of doing something, and a wrong way. And I can always rely on you to choose the wrong way!

The wrong way to deal with clauses is to judge them by their first word. How do you know what part of speech a word is, George?

GEORGE: By the work it does.

TEACHER: Correct. George has remembered Book 2, Lesson 1. Now look at this, Richard. Let us make a clause beginning with your word *where*. Here's a sentence:

The pirates went ⌐where the treasure was hidden.⌐

What kind of a clause is it, Lloyd?

LLOYD: An **adverb clause of place**.

TEACHER: Correct.

RICHARD: But that's what I said!

TEACHER: Listen, Richard. Why is it an **adverb clause**, George?

GEORGE: Because it tells us about the verb *went*. Clauses that limit the meaning of **verbs** are **adverb clauses**.

TEACHER: Very good, George. Now look at this sentence:

The pirates went to the island ⌐where the treasure was hidden.⌐

What kind of a clause is *where the treasure was hidden*, John?

JOHN: I think it's an **adjective clause**.

TEACHER: But it begins with what Richard calls a 'place' word, *where*.

JOHN: That doesn't matter. The clause qualifies the noun *island*; and clauses that qualify or limit the meaning of **nouns** are **adjective clauses**.

TEACHER: And you are quite right, John. I hope you are listening, Richard! Now, here is another sentence:

The pirate told us ⌐where the treasure was hidden.⌐

Harry, what kind of a clause is *where the treasure was hidden*?

HARRY: I think it's a **noun clause**.

TEACHER: But it begins with a 'place' word, *where*. Richard says it's an adverb clause.

HARRY: It isn't. In this case it is the **object** of the verb *told*. If you say, 'The pirate told us, *what*?' the answer is, 'Where the treasure was hidden.' A clause that is the **object** of a **verb** is a **noun clause**.

TEACHER: Quite right, Harry. Did you understand all that, Richard?

RICHARD: Yes, I see now where I was wrong.

27

Lesson Five

Now let us look at those other words that Richard
mentioned, *when*, *who* and *if*. Here are examples of clauses
beginning with these words:

A I shouted with joy | when our school team won the prize. |

B I remember | when our school team won the prize. |

C I remember the day | when our school team won the
prize. |

D Richard is the boy | who scored the winning goal. |

E I asked | who scored the winning goal. |

F George asked me | if Richard had scored a goal. |

G We would all have cheered | if Richard had scored a goal. |

Now write down what kind of clause you think each one is.
When you have tried for yourself, and not until then, look at
the answers on page 30. Remember:

**An adjective clause does the work of an adjective. It qualifies
a noun.**

**An adverb clause does the work of an adverb. It modifies a
verb.** There are adverb clauses of **time, place, manner,
reason, condition, concession.**

**A noun clause does the work of a noun. It is the subject of a
sentence or the object of a verb.**

Exercises

A What kind of clauses are the ones in italics?

1 Tell me *where you are going for your holiday*.
2 The place *where we stayed for our holiday* was right on
the sea coast.
3 I don't know *where we are going this year*.

4 Come *where we are going for our holiday*.
5 Do you know *where Shakespeare was born*?
6 That is the house *where Shakespeare was born*.
7 I don't remember *when Tom came to see me*.
8 I think it was the day *when we had that heavy thunderstorm*.
9 *If that was the day*, it can't be a year ago.
10 I'll ask him *if he remembers the visit*.
11 Tell me *who is coming to the party*.
12 That's one of the boys *who are coming to the party*.

B

You can't please everybody

A man who was going to start a business selling hats wanted a good sign to put over his shop. He chose:

The first friend whose advice he asked said that the word 'hatter' was not needed. *So John crossed out the word 'hatter'*. The next friend he consulted said that it was not necessary to say 'for ready money', because buyers would not expect credit. *So he crossed out 'for ready money'*. The sign now said:

29

Lesson Five

A friend who saw this sign said that when a man bought a hat he didn't ask who made it. *So John crossed out 'makes and'.* But when another friend saw 'John Brown sells hats', he said, 'Of course you sell hats. No one thinks that you give them away.' *So in the end the sign read*:

Analyse the sentences that are NOT in italics. Follow the style on page 24.

Answers to questions on page 28:
A **Adverb clause of time**, modifying the verb *shouted*.
B **Noun clause, object** of the verb *remember*.
C **Adjective clause**, qualifying the noun *day*.
D **Adjective clause**, qualifying the noun *boy*.
E **Noun clause, object** of the verb *asked*.
F **Noun clause, object** of the verb *asked*.
G **Adverb clause of condition**, modifying the verb *would have cheered*.

Did you get them all right?

Lesson Six

Direct and indirect speech: questions

Revision. In **direct speech** we have the exact words of the speaker. In **indirect speech** we have the words of a speaker reported indirectly by another speaker.

When a sentence changes from **direct speech** to **indirect speech**, it is introduced by a verb in the **past tense** (usually *said*). Verbs usually change tense when a sentence is changed from direct to indirect speech.

Pronouns and **possessive adjectives** in the **1st person** or **2nd person** are usually changed to pronouns and possessive adjectives in the **3rd person**.

You have already learned the difference between **direct statements** and **indirect statements** (Book 3, Lesson 21). I now want to explain **direct** and **indirect questions**.

If the direct speech is a question, the indirect speech is introduced by a word like *asked* instead of *said*.

31

Mary said, 'Are you hungry, Margaret?' (direct speech)
Mary asked Margaret if she was hungry. (indirect speech)

Joanna said, 'What do you want, Jane?' (direct speech)
Joanna asked Jane what she wanted. (indirect speech)

TEACHER: Have you all understood me? (direct speech)
The teacher asked the class if they had all understood her.
(indirect speech)

JOHN TO MARY: Shall I close the window? (direct speech)
John asked Mary if he should close the window. (indirect
speech)

Here are some more examples:

Direct question	*Indirect question*
MARGARET (to RICHARD): Where are you going for your holidays?	Margaret asked Richard where he was going for his holidays.
RICHARD (to shopkeeper): What is the price of that bicycle?	Richard asked the shopkeeper what the price of the bicycle was.
George said, 'When will you get back from Kingston, Lance?'	George asked Lance when he would get back from Kingston.
George said, 'How long does it take to get to Kingston, Lance?'	George asked Lance how long it took to get to Kingston.
Richard said, 'Can you swim, John?'	Richard asked John if he could swim.
GEORGE (to teacher): Shall I finish my exercise at home?	George asked the teacher if he should finish his exercise at home.
MARY: May I have another cake, please?	Mary asked if she might have another cake.
JOANNA (to JANE): Do you like my new pen?	Joanna asked Jane if she liked her new pen.

Note the following points:

1 A **direct question** is in the 'question form'. **Verb** ('peculiar') before **subject**. (Book 2, Lesson 18): *Are you . . .?*; *Do you . . .?*; *Have you . . .?*; *Shall I . . .?*

2 An **indirect question** is in the 'statement form'. **Verb** after **subject**: *she was*; *she wanted*; *they had*; *he should*.

3 **Indirect questions** use no question mark.

Notice, too, how in **indirect speech** the meaning may sometimes be ambiguous (not clear). Look at that last sentence:

Joanna asked Jane if she liked her new pen.

Her new pen could mean 'Joanna's new pen' or 'Jane's new pen'. To make the meaning unmistakable it is sometimes necessary to use the rather awkward form:

Joanna asked Jane if she liked her (Joanna's) new pen.

Exercises

A The following sentences use **indirect speech**. Give the actual words (**direct speech**) of the speaker. Don't forget the punctuation. (You may need help with number 4 from Book 2, Lesson 25.)

Example: Mary asked John if he wanted some cake.
Answer: Mary said, 'Do you want some cake, John?'
    or: 'Do you want some cake, John?' asked Mary.
    or: 'Do you want some cake?' Mary asked John.

1 Mrs Lee asked Margaret if she was tired.
2 George asked if they had taken his dog Jock for a walk.
3 The hunter asked if they had heard the sound of wolves.
4 The little girl asked if the baby had a name yet.
5 The passenger inquired what time the train for Bridgetown left.
6 Carl asked William if he had read 'Treasure Island'.

7 The stranger asked where the railway station was.
8 The lady asked Lloyd if he could swim.
9 Richard asked his mother if he might have another piece of cake.
10 John asked Henry if his exercise was correct. (This is ambiguous. Give two answers.)

B Turn the following from **direct speech** to **indirect speech**. We give you some help in brackets.

1 MOTHER TO MARGARET: Have you finished your homework yet? (*asked Margaret if she*)
2 JEREMY: Have you been using my toothpaste, Richard? (*asked Richard if*)
3 Mary said, 'Is your new baby a boy or a girl, Mrs Thompson?' (*if* or *whether*)
4 Elizabeth said, 'Did Margaret feed the cat before she went out?'
5 RICHARD'S MOTHER: Did you brush your teeth properly, Richard? (*asked him*)
6 The hunter said, 'Do you hear the roar of a lion?' (*asked them if they* or *us if we*)
7 The hunter said, 'Did you hear the roar of a lion?'
8 VISITOR (to boy): Do you go to school every day?
9 GEORGE: May I borrow your bicycle, John?
10 STRANGER TO FRED: Can you tell me where Mr Huang lives?

Lesson Seven

Direct and indirect speech: commands

Here are some **direct commands**:
> Open the window.
> Let the man go.
> Stay where you are.

Here are some that are not quite so 'commanding'; they are polite **requests** rather than commands.
> Open the window, please.
> Try a piece of this cake, it's very good.
> Please don't make so much noise.

In **direct commands** and **requests** we use the **base** form of the verb. In **indirect commands** we don't use the **command** form; we use the **base** with *to*.

We introduce the **indirect command** by some word like *told* or *ordered* (for **commands**), *asked* or *begged* (for polite **requests**). Here are some examples:

TEACHER TO STUDENT: Open the window. (direct command)
The teacher told the student to open the window. (indirect command)

The officer said to the soldier, 'Stay where you are.' (direct command)
The officer ordered the soldier to stay where he was. (indirect command)

Don't fire the gun. (direct command)
The officer ordered the soldier not to fire the gun. (indirect command)

Mary said, 'Open the window please, John.' (direct request)
Mary asked John to open the window. (indirect request)

MOTHER TO ROOMFUL OF BOYS: Please don't make so much noise. (direct request)
The mother asked the boys not to make so much noise. (indirect request)

Here are some more examples:

Direct command	Indirect command
TEACHER (to RICHARD): Sit down!	The teacher ordered Richard to sit down.
TEACHER (to HENRY): Clean the blackboard.	The teacher told Henry to clean the blackboard.
The teacher said, 'Come in, George.'	The teacher told George to come in.
MOTHER (to FRED): Please don't eat all the cake.	Mother asked Fred not to eat all the cake.
OFFICER (to soldiers): Fire!	The officer commanded the soldiers to fire.
The teacher said to Richard, 'Do that exercise correctly or you will have to do it again.'	The teacher told Richard to do the exercise correctly or he would have to do it again.
TEACHER: Don't waste your time.	The teacher told the students not to waste their time.
FARMER (to visitors): Please don't leave the gate open.	The farmer asked visitors not to leave the gate open.
Richard's father said, 'Don't climb that tree in your new trousers, Richard.'	Richard's father told him not to climb the tree in his new trousers.

If the direct speech is a command or a request, the indirect speech is introduced by *told*, *ordered*, *asked*.

The base form in the command is changed to *to* + base in the indirect speech.

Don't in the direct command becomes *not to* in the indirect command.

Exercises

A Write the following as **indirect commands** or **requests**:

1 TEACHER TO RICHARD: Write that exercise out carefully.
2 HUNTER TO FRIEND: Shoot the wolf.
3 OFFICER TO SOLDIERS: Bring the gun into position.
4 Mary said to John, 'Open the box for me, please.'

5 Mrs Sangster said, 'Please sing at our party, Joyce.'
6 'Release the prisoners,' said the officer to the sergeant.
7 The captain of the shipwrecked vessel said to the sailors, 'Lower the boats at once.'
8 TEACHER TO GEORGE: Be careful. Think before you answer.
9 RICHARD: Read my exercise, John, and tell me if it is correct.
10 The pirate chief said to the prisoner, 'Look at this map and show me where the treasure is hidden.'

B Here is a short story containing **direct statements**, **questions** and **commands**. Rewrite it in **indirect speech**. Call the ant *he* and the grasshopper *she*.

The Ant and the Grasshopper

It was a cold winter's day, and an ant was bringing out some grains of corn that he had gathered in the summer. He wanted to dry them. A grasshopper, who was very hungry, saw him and said, 'Give me a few grains of corn; I am dying of hunger.'

'But,' said the ant, 'what did you do in the summer? Didn't you store up some corn?'

'No,' replied the grasshopper, 'I was too busy.'

'What did you do?' said the ant.

'I sang all day,' answered the grasshopper.

'If you sang all summer,' said the ant, 'you can dance all winter.'

The infinitive 1

You remember that a **finite verb** has a **subject**, and it can change for **tense** and **person** (Book 2, Lesson 20).

Now we must look at some **non-finite** uses of the **verb**. Let's look again at the table we had in Book 2.

Form	Examples	How we use the form
A Base	pull take put	1 For all the **present tense** except 3rd person singular: I/You/We/ They *pull* the rope. 2 **Commands**: *Pull* that rope. 3 With some 'peculiars': He can *pull* the rope. 4 With *to*: He tried to *pull* the rope.
B -*s* form	pulls takes puts	**3rd person singular, present tense** only: He/She/It/The sailor *pulls* the rope.
C Simple past tense	pulled took put	**Simple past tense**, all persons (Book 2, Lesson 21): He *pulled* the rope an hour ago.
D Past participle	pulled taken put	1 With *have* for the **present perfect tense** (Book 3, Lesson 4): I *have pulled* the rope, and the flag is up.

		2 With *be* for the **passive voice** (Book 3, Lesson 14): That carriage *is pulled* by two horses.
E *-ing* form	pulling taking putting	1 With *be* for the **continuous**: He *is pulling* the rope now. He *wasn't pulling* it an hour ago. 2 Without 'peculiars' (Book 4, Lesson 11): *Pulling* hard, they moved the ship towards them. *Pulling* ropes is hard work.

In this table, A3 and A4 are the **infinitive**. When the **infinitive** of a verb is used with another **verb**, it generally has *to* before it. The finite verbs in these examples are shown in italics, and the infinitives are in boxes.

I *want* to go to Cairo.

Mary *was able* to speak French when she was ten.

They *tried* to find the way to the hotel.

40

But after some **verbs** (shown here in italics) the **infinitive** is the **base** form without *to*. Here are some examples. The words in the boxes are all infinitives.

Mary *can* ⬚ speak ⬚ French.

He *will* ⬚ buy ⬚ a new pen tomorrow.

I *didn't* ⬚ finish ⬚ my homework.

Will you ⬚ lend ⬚ me your book?

I think it *may* ⬚ rain ⬚ .

TEACHER: I said that after some **verbs** there is no *to* before the **infinitive**. Do you notice which verbs they are, John?

JOHN: Yes. They are the 'peculiars'. But do all the 'peculiars' take the infinitive without *to*?

TEACHER: There are three that already have *to*: *ought to*, *have to* and *used to*.

I *ought to* ⬚ warn ⬚ you about that.

You *have to* ⬚ work ⬚ hard to pass this examination.

I *used to* ⬚ eat ⬚ too much.

Exercises

A Copy out the following sentences and draw a box round every **infinitive**.

1 I want to write a letter.
2 I am going to write a letter.
3 Joyce will write a letter too.
4 Shall I write my letter now?
5 Yes, you must write as soon as you can find time.
6 I can't start yet.
7 I know I ought to write much more often.

B Put in a suitable **infinitive** in place of each of these dashes.

1 I should like ____ you.
2 You can't ____ without eyes.
3 They mustn't ____ in the class.
4 They were not allowed ____ in the class.
5 Nobody must ____ my bicycle without permission.
6 You ought not to ____ my bicycle without permission.
7 I want ____ home now.
8 You don't have to ____ home yet.

Lesson Nine

The infinitive 2

You have seen the **infinitive** doing the work of a **verb**, but the infinitive sometimes does the work of a **noun**.

The infinitive as the subject

A **noun** is often the **subject** of a sentence; and so is the **infinitive**. Look at this sentence:
    The sight of Richard's happy face gave me great pleasure.

You remember how to find the subject (see Book 1, Lesson 11). Ask: 'What gave me great pleasure?'
    'The *sight* (noun) of Richard's happy face.'

Alternatively, we can say:
    To see Richard's happy face gave me great pleasure.
'What gave me great pleasure?'
    '*To see Richard's happy face*.' (infinitive phrase)

Here are some more examples where the **infinitive phrase** is the **subject** of the sentence.
    To read a good book is one of the joys of life.
    To make a mistake like that is very careless.
    To learn grammar is not an easy thing.
    To smoke so many cigarettes must be dangerous.

Anticipatory 'it'

There is a very useful construction that saves putting a long **infinitive phrase** at the beginning of a sentence. We use *It*

43

before the **verb**, and then we can have the **infinitive phrase** after the **verb**.

Instead of:
   To see Richard's happy face gave me great pleasure.
we use the *It* construction:
   It gave me great pleasure *to see Richard's happy face*.

Here are some more examples:
   It is very careless *to make a mistake like that*.
   It is not easy *to learn grammar*.
   It must be dangerous *to smoke so many cigarettes*.

The **infinitive** has no **subject**, but with the anticipatory *It* construction we can show the 'doer' of the action with *for*, like this:
   It's good *for a man* to be free.
   It's necessary *for a car* to have a licence.
   It isn't easy *for us* to pay for a new window.
   It wasn't right *for him* to be punished.

In the last two sentences, *we* are going to pay for the window, and *he* was punished, but the pronouns *us* and *him* are **objective** after the **preposition** *for*.

The infinitive as a noun clause

The **infinitive phrase** can even do the work of a **noun clause**. Look at these sentences. Sentences (a) contain **noun clauses**. Sentences (b) have more or less the same meaning but an **infinitive phrase** has taken the place of a **noun clause**.

(a) Do you know *what you have to say*? (noun clause)
(b) Do you know *what to say*? (infinitive phrase)

(a) He asked *if he could see Mr Chung*. (noun clause)
(b) He asked *to see Mr Chung*. (infinitive phrase)

(a) Uncle Arthur promised *that he would give John a bicycle*. (noun clause)
(b) Uncle Arthur promised *to give John a bicycle*. (infinitive phrase)

The infinitive as a complement

You remember that we use the word **complement** to name words or phrases that complete a sentence after verbs like *be* or *seem* (Book 1, Lesson 12). The **infinitive phrase** can be a **complement**:

The best thing is *to say nothing*.
You seem *to have a cold*.

Quite commonly, the **infinitive phrase** is the **complement** of an **adjective**:

He was glad *to be alive*.
I'm very sad *to see such an unhappy child*.
He's silly *to swim so far out*.

Object and infinitive

The **infinitive phrase** is used with an **object** in the form of a **noun** or **pronoun** in sentences like:

He wants everybody to be happy.

Lesson Nine

Here are some more examples. The **object** is in *italics* and the infinitive is in a box.

I asked *him* ⬚to come⬚ as soon as possible.

He told *me* ⬚to go⬚ home.

Richard taught *us* ⬚to swim⬚ .

He forced *me* ⬚to do⬚ the work.

My father allowed *Tom* ⬚to drive⬚ the car.

In sentences of this kind, we don't use *to* after certain verbs. The chief ones are *make, let, hear, see, feel, watch.*

He made *me* ⬚show⬚ him where the treasure was hidden.

They let *us* ⬚join⬚ in the game.

We heard *the burglar* ⬚open⬚ the window, and saw *him* ⬚walk⬚ quickly upstairs.

Tom felt *his heart* ⬚beat⬚ with excitement.

We watched *the bird* ⬚eat⬚ the crumbs.

We could say, then, that the **infinitive** is a 'verb-noun'.
It is like a **noun** because:
1 it can be the **subject** of a sentence,
2 it can be a **complement** or the **object** of a **verb**.

It is like a **verb** because:
1 it expresses an action,
2 it can have an **object**, like this:
> I am trying *to learn* (infinitive) *grammar* (object of infinitive).
> He likes *to read* (infinitive) *a good book* (object of infinitive).
3 it can be modified by an **adverb** (as **verbs** are), like this:
> *To drive* (infinitive) *carefully* (adverb) is better than *to drive* (infinitive) *quickly* (adverb).
> I hope *to see* (infinitive) you *soon* (adverb).

46

Exercises

A Rewrite the following sentences using an **infinitive** instead of the words in *italics*.

Example: He likes *the sight of* people enjoying themselves.
Answer: He likes *to see* people enjoying themselves.

1 I like *a walk* along the sea-shore.
2 The shipwrecked sailors were overjoyed *at the sight of* land.
3 *Truthfulness* is sometimes more difficult than *winning* a battle.
4 I was glad *at the sound of* his voice.
5 I should be sorry *if I heard* that you couldn't do this exercise.
6 Richard was told *that he must not touch* the cakes.
7 Mr Shah asked *if he could see* the headmaster.
8 I was very sorry *when I heard* that you had had an accident.
9 Richard said that he did not expect *that he would get* all the exercise right.
10 The boys laughed *when they saw* the comical tricks of the clown.

B Change these sentences to use an **infinitive** construction after anticipatory *It*.

Example: To be a really good tennis player was her one ambition.
Answer: It was her one ambition to be a really good tennis player.

1 To see you again after all this time is wonderful.
2 To see you again after all this time will be wonderful.
3 Not to go to the cinema would be foolish.
4 To think that all people are greedy is wrong.
5 To whip a horse like that is very cruel.

6 For James to guess her age is impossible.
7 For him to pay for all of us is not right.
8 For us not to help each other wouldn't be right.
9 Not to keep some food for tomorrow would be stupid.
10 Our fathers said that to die for one's country was truly noble.

The *–ing* form: participles

Revision. The **present participle** is the form of the verb that ends in *-ing*. The present participle is used with the verb *be* to form the continuous tenses (E 1 in the table on page 40 of this book).

The **past participle** of **regular verbs** is made by adding *-d, -ed* or *-t* to the **base** of the verb. The past participle of **irregular verbs** is made by changing the vowel (Book 2, Lesson 22). The **past participle** is used with the verb *have* to form the **present perfect tense** (D 1 in the table on page 39 and Book 3, Lesson 4) and with *be* for the **passive** (D 2 and Book 3, Lesson 14).

Present participles

TEACHER: Here are some **present participles**:
    The *running* horse galloped down the road.
    Listen to that *singing* bird.
  What work is *running* doing there, Richard?
RICHARD: It is telling us about the noun *horse*.
TEACHER: Correct. And what work is *singing* doing there, Lance?
LANCE: It qualifies the noun *bird*.
TEACHER: Quite right. And what do we call words that qualify **nouns**?
JAMES: Adjectives.
TEACHER: Very good, James. But these words *singing* and

running are also partly **verbs**. They are part of the verbs *sing* and *run*. *Singing* and *running* are **present participles**.

Past participles

The **past participles** can do exactly the same work. Look at these examples:

There was some *broken* glass on the road.

Those are *stolen* goods.

Brightly *coloured* pictures hung on the wall.

Broken, stolen, coloured are parts of the verbs *break, steal, colour*. They are **past participles**. Here they are doing the work of **adjectives** in qualifying the nouns *glass, goods*, and *pictures*.

So, you see, a **participle** does something of the work of a **verb** and something of the work of an **adjective**. If we were doing mathematics we might write it like this:

PARTICIPLE = VERB + ADJECTIVE
$$P = V + A$$

A participle is partly a verb and partly an adjective.

Exercises

A Give the **present participle** and the **past participle** of the following verbs:

1 walk	6 freeze	11 run	16 tie
2 choose	7 hang	12 begin	17 lay
3 dig	8 ride	13 break	18 write
4 fight	9 ring	14 buy	19 fall
5 forgive	10 rise	15 come	20 fly

B What work does a **participle** do? What is the meaning of $P = V + A$.

C Make sentences to show the use of *-ing* forms with *am, is, are, was, were*.

Example: I am eating an apple.

D Make sentences to show the use of **past participles** with *has, have, had, is, are, was, were*.

Example: Some boys have taken our picnic.

E Write down the **present participles** in the following sentences and show that they are being used as **adjectives**. You can do this by pointing out the **noun** that each one qualifies.

Example: We found the missing piece of the jigsaw.
Answer: The adjective 'missing' qualifies the noun 'piece'.

1 I know the missing word in that sentence.
2 The hero was welcomed home by cheering crowds.
3 I don't like to see singing birds in cages.
4 The boy took a flying leap into the water.
5 I saw the man walking down the street.
6 The man led a dancing bear on a chain.
7 I was kept awake by a barking dog.
8 The rushing wind roared in our ears.
9 The teacher told us an amusing story.
10 The boy came running out of the house.

Lesson Eleven

The -*ing* form: gerunds

TEACHER: In the last lesson we looked at the **present participle**, the part of the verb that ends in -*ing* and is partly a **verb** and partly an **adjective**.

Now look at these sentences:
1 *Running* is my favourite sport.
2 *Seeing* is *believing*.
3 *Crying* won't help matters.
4 *Speaking* a language every day is the best way of *learning* it.
5 I like to hear good *singing*.
6 Our house needs *painting*.
7 I hate *losing* my temper.
8 I don't remember *seeing* you before.
9 You won't do any good by *crying*.
10 The girl was praised for *doing* her work neatly.
11 Richard is fond of *swimming* in deep water.
12 You can't live without *eating*.

What work is being done by *running, seeing, crying, speaking* (sentences 1, 2, 3, 4), Wayne?

WAYNE: They are all names of actions. They are the **subjects** of sentences. They are doing the work of **nouns**.

TEACHER: Quite right, Wayne. Now look at sentences 5, 6, 7, 8. What work is being done by *singing, painting, losing, seeing*, George?

GEORGE: I think they are **objects** of **verbs**. They are doing the work of **nouns**.

TEACHER: Very good, George. Now, Mark, look at sentences 9, 10, 11, 12. What do you notice about the words *crying, doing, swimming, eating*?

MARK: They are all the names of something. They are like **nouns**.

TEACHER: Quite true. In fact in some of them you could put an ordinary **noun** instead of the word ending in -*ing*. For example:

9 You won't do any good by *tears* (crying).
10 The girl was praised for *neatness* (doing her work neatly).
12 You can't live without *food* (eating).

Did you notice, too, that they were all governed by **prepositions**:

by crying
for doing
of swimming
without eating?

And you know that **prepositions** generally govern **nouns**. So quite plainly these words, as used in these sentences, are partly **nouns**.

But they are also partly **verbs**. They express an action. Besides, if they are formed from **transitive verbs** they take **objects**, just as **verbs** do.

I hate ⎡ losing ⎤ my *temper*.

⎡ Speaking ⎤ a *language* every day is the best way of ⎡ learning ⎤ *it*.

The girl was praised for ⎡ doing ⎤ her *work* neatly.

I don't remember ⎡ seeing ⎤ *you* before.

These -*ing* forms are partly **verbs** and partly **nouns**. They are not participles. They are **gerunds**. Let's have a **gerund** formula: G = V + N.

A gerund is the part of a verb ending in -*ing* that is partly a verb and partly a noun.

A gerund can be the subject of a sentence or the object of a verb, or it may be governed by a preposition.

If a gerund is formed from a transitive verb it can take an object.

GERUND

PRESENT PARTICIPLE

WE LOOK ALIKE BUT OUR WORK IS DIFFERENT

Exercises

A What is the meaning of G = V + N?

B Point out the **gerunds** in the following sentences and give the function of each (ie the work each is doing). Say whether it is the **subject** of a sentence, the **object** of a **verb** or governed by a **preposition**.

Example: I like to watch good dancing.
Answer: dancing – object of verb.

1 Swimming is a very enjoyable exercise.
2 I like swimming very much.
3 John is fond of swimming but Louis prefers dancing.
4 Every Friday afternoon we have singing.
5 Richard doesn't like singing very much.
6 We use a knife and fork for eating meat.
7 You will only succeed by trying hard.
8 Mr Green likes gardening, but he doesn't like cutting the grass.

9 I don't want to force you into doing something against your will.

10 Richard hates getting up early in the morning.

C Say which of the words in italics are **gerunds** and which are **present participles**.

1 The *retreating* army took up new positions.

2 They hated *retreating* before the enemy, but by *retreating* they avoided capture.

3 By *working* hard he hopes to get the garden ready for *sowing* seeds.

4 'There was a *rustling* that seemed like a *bustling*.
  Small feet were pattering, wooden shoes were clattering,
  Little hands clapping and little tongues chattering.
  Out came the children *running*.
  All the little boys and girls,
  With *sparkling* eyes and teeth like pearls,
  Tripping and *skipping*, ran merrily after
  The wonderful music with *shouting* and laughter.'

(From the Pied Piper of Hamelin by Robert Browning.)

Apposition

Written English (not so much spoken English) uses **apposition** frequently. Here is an example of apposition in its simplest form:

John Williams, the guitar player, is coming to Manchester.

The expression *the guitar player* is said to be **in apposition** to *John Williams*. In the simplest form of apposition, you can leave out either of the two equal parts:

John Williams is coming to Manchester.
The guitar player is coming to Manchester.

Here are some more examples of **apposition**:

Our neighbours, Mr and Mrs Huang, are very friendly.
An unusual present, a bag of flour, came in the post.
Tennis, her only interest, has brought her many friends.

Sometimes we use the **infinitive** in **apposition**:

His one ambition, to score a goal for England, won't be realized now.

That example is not of the simplest form of **apposition**. We can leave out the **infinitive** phrase, and say:

His ambition won't be realized now.

But we wouldn't normally say or write:

~~To score a goal for England won't be realized now.~~

Restrictive and non-restrictive

The examples of **apposition** that we have had so far are **non-restrictive**. In

John Williams, the guitar player

we are reminding the hearer or reader of what John Williams is famous for, but we are not restricting the meaning of his name. On the other hand, suppose the person we are speaking to has an aunt, a sister and a cousin, all called 'Jane', we might say:

Jane your cousin was here this morning.

And the phrase in apposition, *your cousin*, would be **restrictive** because we are distinguishing the particular *Jane* we mean.

Here are some more examples of **restrictive apposition**. Notice the punctuation (no commas).

My friend Alison was here last night.

The decision to buy the car took a little time. (infinitive in apposition)

The question whether to buy it or not worried us. (infinitive in apposition)

The explanation that he couldn't see it seems very improbable. (noun clause in apposition)

In all the examples so far, the two expressions **in apposition** have been **subjective**. But apposition can be **objective**:

I won't believe *the explanation that he didn't see it*. (noun clause in apposition)

His father supported *the decision to buy the car*. (infinitive in apposition)

The two expressions can be governed by a **preposition**:

They live *in Jamaica, that pleasant Caribbean island*. (non-restrictive)

It is a present *for my friend Peter*. (restrictive)

And finally, they can also be separated by other parts of the sentence:

An unusual present came in the afternoon post, *a book on grammar*.

His ambition is quite clear, *to play football for England*.

57

Exercises

A Add one of the expressions (*a* to *j*) to each sentence (1 to 10), **in apposition** to an expression already in the sentence.

Example: 1 j. Paris, the capital of France, is a very beautiful city.

a 'your cousin'
b the Thais
c the price of a railway ticket to London
d Mary
e George Washington
f to sell his car
g the film actor
h an old Rolls Royce
i Marilyn Monroe
j the capital of France.

1 Paris is a very beautiful city.
2 The phrase in apposition is restrictive.
3 John Wayne sometimes visited London.
4 I'm very fond of George's sister.
5 I suppose we can afford £8.50.
6 It was very sad about the beautiful star.
7 What do you think of his decision?
8 He is always boasting about his car.
9 What do you know about the people of Thailand?
10 The first President of the United States died in 1799.

B In each sentence, one expression is printed in italics. Find the expression that is **in apposition** to it, and write it in Column 1. Then fill in Columns 2 to 4. The answer to number 1 is already completed.

1 Expression in apposition	2 Noun phrase or noun clause or infinitive	3 Restrictive or non-restrictive	4 Subjective or objective
Jack Land	Noun phrase	Restrictive	Subjective

1 *The football referee* Jack Land often sent players off the field.
2 They respected *his last wish*, to be buried next to his wife.
3 *His last wish*, that they should bury him next to his wife, was respected.
4 *The dish* was already on the table, fish and chips.
5 *Your brother* William is a bit crazy, isn't he?
6 *The writer* C.E. Eckersley lived here.
7 What do you think of *the decision* to build a hotel here?
8 *His explanation* that he couldn't see it didn't please them.
9 What do you think of *his idea* that the world is flat?

Conditions: open and hypothetical

Open condition

In the lesson on **adverb clauses**, you met some **adverb clauses of condition**, clauses like these:

If Richard works hard, he will learn grammar.

I'll help him *if he asks me*.

These clauses simply mean: 'If Richard works, he will learn; if he doesn't work, he won't learn.' 'If he asks me, I'll help him; if he doesn't ask me, I won't help him.'

Richard has the choice between 'working' and 'not working'. He has the choice between 'asking' and 'not asking'. These are what we call **open conditions**.

In an open condition we have the simple present tense in the *if*-clause. In the main clause we have the future tense.

Hypothetical condition

But there is another kind of condition – **hypothetical condition**. *Hypothetical* means 'not yet proved to be true'. Here are some examples set side by side with **open conditions**.

Open condition	*Hypothetical condition*
If Richard works hard, he will learn grammar.	If Richard worked hard, he would learn grammar.
I will help him if he asks me.	I would help him if he asked me.

He will do the work if he has time.	He would do the work if he had time.
I'll go for a walk if the rain stops.	I would go for a walk if the rain stopped.
What will you do if I give you the choice?	What would you do if I gave you the choice?
We will help you if you need help.	We would help you if you needed help.
I'll speak if I am sure of the answer.	I would speak if I were sure of the answer.

TEACHER: Do you notice anything about all those hypothetical sentences, Lance? Look at the first one.

LANCE: Well, the present tense *works* has changed to the past tense *worked*, and *will learn* has changed to *would learn*.

TEACHER: Yes, that's quite true, and there is a reason for the difference. In the **open condition**,

If Richard works hard, he will learn grammar.

we don't know whether Richard will work hard. Perhaps he will work hard. Then he will learn grammar. Perhaps he won't work hard. Then he won't learn grammar. We *don't know*.

In the **hypothetical condition**,

If Richard worked hard, he would learn grammar.

we don't really suppose that Richard will work hard. Probably he won't work hard. So he won't learn grammar.

In a hypothetical condition we use the simple past tense in the *if*-clause. In the main clause we use *would* and the base form of the verb.

Unless

Unless Richard works hard, he won't learn grammar. *Unless* means *if . . . not*, but when we use it there is a difference:

61

You will hurt yourself *if you are not careful*.
– so be careful.
You will hurt yourself *unless you are careful*.
– so it would be better not to do it at all.

Exercises

A Which of the following are **open conditions** and which are **hypothetical conditions**?

1 If it is not foggy tomorrow, we will come.
2 If I saw him, I would speak to him.
3 I would play football if you asked me.
4 If the weather men are right, it's going to rain this evening.
5 If you gave that answer, you would be wrong.
6 If he spoke to me, I would speak to him.
7 If he asked for money, would you give him any?
8 Will you give him money if he asks for it?
9 If it were not so foggy, we would play football.
10 If he feels hungry, he will eat his dinner.

B Change the following from **open conditions** to **hypothetical conditions**.

Example: If I have time, I will help you.
Answer: If I had time, I would help you.

1 If he asks me, I will play football.
2 I'll speak to him if he speaks to me.
3 If he listens to what I say, he won't make silly mistakes.
4 If the sun comes out, the rain will soon stop.
5 He will open the box if he can find the key.
6 If he feels hungry, he will eat his dinner.
7 If I begin the work, I know he will finish it.
8 If you feed the baby properly, she will soon be well.

Lesson Fourteen

Past conditions

In the last lesson we saw the **past tense** in the **hypothetical condition**.

Open condition
If Richard works hard, he will learn grammar.
We will help you if you need help.
He will do the work if he has time.

Hypothetical condition
If Richard *worked* hard, he would learn grammar.
We would help you if you *needed* help.
He would do the work if he *had* time.

In the **hypothetical conditions** the past tense *worked* was used instead of the present tense *works*, and *would learn* was used instead of *will learn*.

Well, the funny thing is that, though we use a *past* tense, the meaning is really a *present* one. The **hypothetical conditions** mean:

   . . . if he worked hard *now* (but he doesn't work hard *now*).
   . . . if you needed help *now* (but you don't need help *now*).
   . . . if he had time *now* (but he doesn't have time *now*).

We can have **hypothetical conditions** in past time, too. Here is how we would express the **past conditions**. As you will see we use the **past perfect** (*had* + **past participle**) in the *if*-**clause**, and *would have* + **past participle** in the **main clause**.

   Richard *would have learned* grammar if he *had worked* hard (but he didn't work hard *in the past* – and he didn't learn *in the past*).

63

We *would have helped* you if you *had needed* help (but you didn't).

He *would have done* the work if he *had had* time (but he didn't have time).

Here are some further examples of these three constructions to help you to understand them:

Open condition: If the master pays him properly, the workman will work well. (Perhaps it will happen.)

Hypothetical condition: If the master paid him properly, the workman would work well. (Probably it won't happen.)

Past condition: If the master had paid him properly, the workman would have worked well. (But neither of these things happened.)

Open condition: If these stamps are genuine, they will be worth a lot of money. (Perhaps they are.)

Hypothetical condition: If these stamps were genuine, they would be worth a lot of money. (Probably they aren't genuine.)

Past condition: If these stamps had been genuine, they would have been worth a lot of money. (But they weren't genuine.)

Open condition: If you tell me what you want, I'll buy you a present. (Perhaps it will happen.)

Hypothetical condition: If you told me what you wanted, I would buy you a present. (But you haven't told me – yet.)

Past condition: If you had told me what you wanted, I would have bought you a present. (But you didn't tell me, and so you didn't get a present.)

In a past condition we have the past perfect tense in the *if*-clause. In the main clause we have *would have* and a past participle.

This summary of a rather difficult matter may help you:

	Main clause	*if-clause*
Open condition	He will learn	if he works. (simple present)
Hypothetical condition	He would learn	if he worked. (simple past)
Past condition	He would have learned	if he had worked. (past perfect)

Exercise

Turn these sentences (a) into **hypothetical conditions** (b) into **past conditions**.

Example: If you do that, you will be all right.
Answer: (a) If you did that, you would be all right.
        (b) If you had done that, you would have been all right.

1 If the cat is hungry, I will give it some food.
2 If it rains, the garden-party will be spoiled.
3 If you leave now, you will catch the train.
4 Ali will pass his examination if he works.
5 I will give him the money if I see him.
6 If you drink that, it will kill you.
7 The boy will post your letter if you give it to him.

Lesson Fifteen

Modal auxiliaries 1

There are some **verbs** (and as you might expect, they are 'peculiars') that have certain parts missing. They are **modal auxiliaries**. We use them with other **verbs**, not alone unless a part of another verb is 'understood'. Here are some examples:

'*Can* you *see* that ship?' – 'Yes, I *can*.' (Meaning: '*can see* it')

'I *can do* it.' – 'Oh, *can* you?' (Meaning: '*can* you *do* it')

Can

Can has only two forms, the present *can* and the past *could*. *Can* means *be able to*. For example you can say:

Can you speak French?

OR *Are* you *able to* speak French?

Richard *could* swim when he was six years old.

OR Richard *was able to* swim when he was six years old.

Can has no **future** form or **past participle** or **infinitive**, so instead it uses some form of *be able to*:

I'*ll be able to* (future) do this exercise now that you have explained it.

Richard has *been able to* (past participle) swim for six years.

I hope *to be able to* (infinitive) come to the party tonight.

May

May, too, has only two forms, *may* and *might*.

1 *May* is often used to ask permission.

JOHN: *May* I borrow your bicycle, Tom?

MARGARET AND MARY: *May* we go into your garden, Mr Green?

Quite often, as a matter of fact, we use *can* to ask permission.

Can I borrow your bicycle?

Can we go into your garden?

But *I can* really means *I am able to*. *I may* means *I am allowed to*. Some people are (perhaps rather unnecessarily) strict about this. You will see that in this little conversation.

YOUNG NEPHEW: *Can* I smoke in your sitting-room, Aunt?

STRICT OLD AUNT: You *can*, Charles, but you *may* not.

If we want to put these sentences into the past we use the modal auxiliary *might*.

John asked if he *might* borrow Tom's bicycle.

Margaret and Mary asked if they *might* go into Mr Green's garden.

Charles asked his aunt if he could smoke. She said that he could but that he *might* not.

For the missing parts of *may* we do as we did with *can*: we use another verb (generally *allow* or *let*).

John *may* (present) borrow my bicycle.

Tom said John *might* (past) borrow his bicycle.

Tom has *allowed* (past participle) John *to* borrow his
bicycle.
Tom has *let* (past participle) John borrow his bicycle.
Tom *will allow* (future) John *to* borrow his bicycle.
Tom *will let* (future) John borrow his bicycle.
I *am allowing* (present continuous) John *to* borrow my
bicycle.
I *am letting* (present continuous) John borrow my bicycle.

2 **Sometimes *may* (or *might*) expresses another meaning:
possibility.** You will see that meaning in these examples:
MARY AND MARGARET: We want to have a picnic this
afternoon, Mother. Do you think it's going to rain?
MOTHER: Well, it *may* rain; there are some clouds in the
sky. But the sun *may* come out and clear them away.

And here's what the girls said the next morning, talking of
their picnic:
'Before we went for our picnic we asked mother if she
thought it *might* rain. She said it *might* because there were
clouds in the sky, but she hoped the sun *might* come out
and clear the clouds away. And I'm glad to say it did, and
we had a lovely picnic.'

Exercises

A What are the two meanings of: 'I may go with you to the
cinema'?

B In the following sentences replace *can* or *could* by the
necessary *be able to* form:

Example: Could you see the sea from your camp?
Answer: Were you able to see the sea from your camp?

 1 Richard can swim well.
 2 I could hear every word you said.

3 I couldn't hear a word you said.
4 Henry can lift that heavy box.
5 Jan couldn't lift that heavy box.
6 We can't do all these exercises in five minutes.
7 I can just hear what he says. (*am just able to*)
8 I could just hear what he said.
9 What time tomorrow can I see you? (*tomorrow suggests a future time.*)
10 Can you see me tomorrow?

C Make the following sentences refer to (a) the **past**, (b) the **future**. Add any necessary 'time' expressions.

Example: Can you play tennis?
Answer: (a) Could you play tennis as a child?
       (b) Will you be able to play tennis when you are 60?

1 He can stay here for an hour.
2 You can do this exercise quite easily.
3 I can write to him because I have his address.
4 I can't write to him because I haven't got his address.
5 We can't understand him because he speaks English so badly.

D Write sentences that mean the same as the following but using *can*, *could*, *may*, *might*, or their negative forms with *n't*.

Example: She wasn't able to lift the box because she was old.
Answer: She couldn't lift the box because she was old.

1 My eyes are good, and I am able to see for miles.
2 Will you allow me to have another sandwich, please?
3 What would we be able to see if the mist cleared?
4 It was possible for us to see the sea before they built that house.
5 Will you let me play your piano?
6 It is impossible for us to see the sea from here.

Lesson Sixteen

Modal auxiliaries 2

The **modal auxiliary** *must* has only that one form. It has no
infinitive, no past tense, no future and no participles. But
let us look at its meaning.

Must as a command

**The main meaning of *must* suggests a command or an
obligation.**
  Richard *must* finish his work before he goes home.
  You *must* write your exercise neatly.
  I *must* try hard to understand this lesson.

Or, in the **negative**:
  You *mustn't* play football in the street.
  People *must not* try to feed these animals.
  I *mustn't* go to sleep in the grammar lesson.

Sometimes the opposite of *must* is *must not* (*mustn't*) and
sometimes it is *need not* (*needn't*). Here is a short
conversation to illustrate this:

HENRY: We are having a party at our house tomorrow, Mary.
  It begins at four o'clock. Will you come?
MARY: Thank you very much. I'd like to come, but we have
  school in the afternoon. *Must* I come at four o'clock?
HENRY: Oh no, you *needn't* come at four, but you *mustn't* be
  too late or all the best food may be gone.
MARY: But I *must* go home first to put on another dress.

HENRY: Oh, you *needn't* do that. You'll be late if you do. The dress you are wearing is very nice.

MARY: Oh yes, I *must* change my dress, but you *needn't* worry, I won't be very late. I'll be there by half-past four.

Use *mustn't* when the meaning suggests a command. Use *needn't* when the meaning is 'It isn't necessary'.

Here is one more example:

You *must* (affirmative) give the man £2 (two pounds).
You *mustn't* (negative) give the man £2. (Don't do it.)
You *needn't* (negative) give the man £2. (It isn't necessary, but you can do as you please, give it or not give it.)

We can't use *will* with *must*. So to express the **future** we use *have to*:

I'*ll have to* see the dentist tomorrow about my bad tooth.
They *will have to* run if they want to catch the train.

For the **past** we use *had to*:

I *had to* go to the dentist yesterday about my bad tooth.
They *had to* run to catch the train.

Another meaning

There is another meaning of *must* that suggests not compulsion, but rather what seems reasonable.

You have worked hard all day, so you *must* be tired.
George *must* be pleased that he has passed his examination.
If John left here at four o'clock, he *must* be home by now.

The opposite of this particular *must* is usually *can't*:

You haven't done any work today, so you *can't* be tired.
George can't be very pleased about his low marks.
John left here only five minutes ago; he *can't* be home yet.

Exercises

A What are the two main meanings of *must*? Give an example of each.

B Put *mustn't* or *needn't* in the blank spaces. Choose the one that seems to you the more suitable.

1 You ____ do the work this evening; tomorrow will be soon enough.
2 I told him that he ____ say those silly things.
3 You ____ sit there in your wet clothes; you will catch cold if you do.
4 They ____ do all the exercises. Four will be enough.
5 We ____ go just yet. Our train doesn't leave for half an hour.

C Put the following sentences into the **past**. Make any necessary alterations to 'time phrases'.

Example: I want to know if I must start now.
Answer: I wanted to know if I had to start at once.

1 I must give an answer at once.
2 We must clear away the snow before we can get to the gate.
3 I must read to the end of the story because I want to see who gets the treasure.
4 Carmen must not open the box of chocolates until her sister comes home.
5 They must leave the house because the new owner wants to come in.

The 'peculiars': auxiliary verbs 1

Revision (Book 2, Lessons 15–18). There are a number of 'peculiars': *be, have, can/could, do, shall/should, will/would, may, might, must, need, ought to, dare, used to.*

They are the only **verbs** that form their **negative** by adding *not* only.

They are the only verbs that form their **interrogative** by **inversion**, and the only ones that use 'contracted forms'.

They are all, if you include *ought to* and *used to*, followed by the **infinitive** without *to* (see Lesson 8).

You have already seen some of the work that the 'peculiars' do. They like to be helpful. For example, *do* helps other **verbs** to form the **interrogative**.

  Do you like chocolate?
  Did you offer Mary some chocolate?
It helps, too, to form the **negative**.
  I *do* not (don't) like chocolate.
  I *did* not (didn't) offer Mary any chocolate.

Other 'peculiars' help to make **tenses**:
  I *have eaten* my chocolate. (present perfect)
  I *had eaten* it before you came. (past perfect)
  I *was eating* chocolate during the lesson. (past continuous)
  Richard *is eating* some now. (present continuous)
  I *will* (I'*ll*) *keep* this chocolate until after the lesson.
  (future)
  I *will have eaten* it all by tomorrow. (future perfect)

Others again help verbs to form the **passive voice** (Book 3, Lesson 15):

The thief *will be caught.*

The thief *was caught.*

The thief *has been caught.*

Would helps to express **hypothetical conditions**:

Richard *would learn* grammar if he worked hard.

I *would be* happy if I could go to London

and **past conditions**:

Richard *would have passed* the exam if he had worked harder.

Because these verbs (*be, have, do, will*, etc.) help other verbs they are called **auxiliary** or 'helping' **verbs**.

Exercises

A Give examples of an **auxiliary verb**:

(a) forming a **negative**,   (b) forming an **interrogative**,
(c) forming a **tense**,   (d) forming the **passive**.

B Here is a short story:

Three cheers for the Navy!

Jack, an old sailor who had spent many years in the Navy, was walking along a country road when he came to a farm house. The farmer was standing at the door and Jack said, 'I have been walking all day looking for work. Will you give me a job?'

'Have you ever done any farm work?' said the farmer.

'No,' said Jack. 'I have been a sailor all my life, but I will do any job you like to give me.'

'All right,' said the farmer. 'I'll give you a chance. Do you see that flock of sheep scattered over the hillside?'

'Yes,' answered Jack.

'Well,' said the farmer. 'Get them all through that gate and into the yard.'

'Right,' said Jack. 'I'll do that.'

About an hour later the farmer went to the yard. Jack was leaning on the gate wiping his forehead.

'Did you get them all in?' said the farmer.

'Yes,' said Jack. The farmer looked and sure enough all the sheep were gathered in the yard. And then the farmer saw a hare running round among the sheep. The sailor saw what he was looking at.

'Yes,' he said, 'that little fellow there gave me more trouble than all the other sheep.'

Pick out all the **auxiliaries** (there are 16) and say what work each one is doing. For example, in the first sentence, *had* is helping to form the past perfect *had spent*.

Lesson Eighteen

The 'peculiars': auxiliary verbs 2

We will begin this lesson with a 'rule'.

We use auxiliary verbs with other verbs, not alone unless a part of another verb is 'understood'.

will   I will *help* (infinitive) you.
do   I don't *know* (infinitive) your friend.
are   We are *learning* (present participle) grammar.
have   We have *learned* (past participle) about present and past participles.

JOHN: But what about the verb *do* in this sentence?
    The gardener *did* his work well.
Did is used alone there; there isn't any part of another verb, or any 'understood' part.

TEACHER: Well done, John. I hoped someone would bring up that point. The explanation is this. Three of the 'peculiars' (*be, have* and *do*) 'lead a double life'. Sometimes they are 'peculiars' and act like 'peculiars', and sometimes they are ordinary verbs and act like all the other verbs. When they are ordinary verbs they don't need another verb to complete them. They are 'full' verbs and can make a predicate by themselves. Let me show you examples.

    1 *be, have* and *do* as **auxiliary verbs**:
        I *am* teaching grammar.
        I *have* taught grammar.
        Do you understand this lesson?

As you can see, the verbs in italics are used with a **nonfinite** (Book 2, Lesson 20). These verbs are used here as **auxiliaries**.

2 *be, have* and *do* as **full verbs**:
I *am* the teacher.
'To be or not to be, that *is* the question.' (Shakespeare)
The party *was* last night.
I *have* a new book.
We *had* a good dinner today.
The gardener *did* his work well.

Dare and *used to*

Here are some examples of *dare* and *used to*:
   Dare you climb (infinitive without *to*) that tree?
   I *daren't* climb it.
   Used you *to* climb that tree when you were a boy?
   Yes, I *used to* climb it when I was a boy.
   I *usedn't* (pronounced *usen't*) *to* be afraid then.
Notice these verbs act like 'peculiars': (a) They make their
negative by using simply *not* (*n't*); (b) They make their
interrogative by **inversion**.

But they can also make their **interrogative** and **negative** as all
verbs except the 'peculiars' do, by using *do* and *do not*.
   Did you *dare* to ask for another exercise book?
   I *didn't dare* to ask for another exercise book. My present
   one was not full.
   Did you *use to* climb trees when you were a boy?
   I *didn't use to* be afraid then.

Need

There is one more verb that leads a double life in this way:
need. It is a 'peculiar' in sentences like:
   You *needn't* feel worried. It's quite easy.
But sometimes it is a full verb:
   Your exercise book isn't full. You *don't need* a new one.

77

Exercise

What is a **full verb**? In which of the following sentences are the verbs *be, do, need* and *have* used as **auxiliaries**? In which are they **full verbs**?

Example: Did you finish your homework last night? I always do mine after supper.

Answer: Did – auxiliary. do – full verb.

1 I did all my exercises correctly yesterday.
2 Did George get all his exercises correct?
3 What time does the lesson start?
4 Have you read this new book?
5 I have a copy of it at home but I haven't read it yet.
6 I want to move this table and I need your help.
7 You needn't come at once if you are busy; we can do the job later.
8 We have a big table like this. We need a big one for our family.
9 What time is the football match? Is Richard playing in it?
10 We have been doing some painting, but we need some more paint. Have you any red paint that you are not using?

Lesson Nineteen

The 'peculiars':
the emphatic form

You have already been told a number of the peculiarities of
the 'peculiars', but there are quite a number of other things
that you have not yet been told.

Sometimes when we are speaking, we want to be emphatic;
that is, we want to put the matter rather more strongly. In
speaking, we can do this by saying a particular word with
more force. In writing we sometimes do this by underlining
the word or printing it in italics, like this:

He thought I was not listening, but I *was* listening.
You think Mary is not clever, but she *is* clever.
Richard says I can't climb that tree, but I *can* climb it.
I don't want to say this, but I *must* say it.
You believed the cat hadn't stolen the meat, but it *had*.
I don't want to punish the cat, but I *will* punish it.
What can he mean by saying that? It *cannot* be true.

**But the only verbs that we can emphasize like this are the
'peculiars'.**

Suppose we want to emphasize a verb that is not one of the
'peculiars'. What do we do then?

Here is a little conversation that I expect you have heard
several times before between Richard and me.

TEACHER: Richard, you must try hard with your grammar.
RICHARD (*feeling that I am being unfair*): But I *do* try hard
with my grammar.
TEACHER: You didn't try with the last exercise I gave you.

RICHARD: I *did* try hard with it.
TEACHER: I don't think you took much care with it.
RICHARD: Oh yes, I *did* take care with it.
TEACHER: You don't spend much time on the work.
RICHARD: Oh I *do* spend a lot of time on it.

Do you notice how Richard emphasized the verbs *try, take, spend*?

When the teacher said:
'You don't try,' the unemphatic answer would be 'I try'.
'You didn't try,' the unemphatic answer would be 'I tried'.
'You didn't take much care,' the unemphatic answer
would be 'I took care'.
'You don't spend,' the unemphatic answer would be 'I
spend'.

But Richard changed the answer from
'I try'	into	'I *do* try'.
'I spend'	"	'I *do* spend'.
'I tried'	"	'I *did* try'.
'I took'	"	'I *did* take'.

**The emphatic form of the verb is made by changing the finite
verb into the infinitive and putting *do* (one of the 'peculiars')
before it.**

Here are some examples:

Unemphatic	*Emphatic*
Present tense	
I like chocolate	I *do* like chocolate.
He hates being late for school.	He *does* hate being late for school.
George works hard.	George *does* work hard.
Command	
Sit down.	*Do* sit down.
Past tense	
Louis cooked a good dinner.	Louis *did* cook a good dinner.
You sang that song well.	You *did* sing that song well.

Exercises

A Say the following sentences, stressing one of the **verbs** in each in order to make the sentences emphatic:

1 Elizabeth can play the piano well.
2 William is a big boy for his age.
3 I will be glad to be home again.
4 We were sorry you had to go so early.
5 You will try to come again, won't you?
6 I must get this work done before Friday.

B Write the following sentences in the emphatic form:

1 Richard likes cakes.
2 He enjoyed the ones he ate at the party.
3 I like the cakes that Mrs King bakes.
4 We had a good swim this afternoon.
5 You bought a lot of chocolate.
6 Richard runs fast.

7 The wind blew hard when we were at sea.

8 You brought a lot of clothes with you.

9 Henry came here quickly.

10 Henry comes here quickly.

11 Richard drank a lot of lemonade.

12 They took a long time to come here.

13 Those shoes I bought wore well.

14 He promised he would write and he wrote.

15 It froze hard last night.

16 You told me to see the picture at the cinema and I saw it.

17 He asked me to teach him French and I taught him.

18 The cook makes the food taste good.

The 'peculiars': question tags

You have noticed, I expect, those little **question tags** that we often use in conversation. Instead of asking a question directly, we make a statement and put a **question tag** at the end. This is what I mean:

He is Jamaican, *isn't he*? (question tag)
You were there, *weren't you*? (question tag)

The verb in the question tag is always in the same tense as the verb in the statement.

In the first example above, the verb in the **statement** is present tense, *is*. The verb in the **question tag** is present tense, *isn't*.

In the second example, the verb is in the past tense, *were*; so the verb in the question tag is past tense, *weren't*.

If the statement is positive, the question tag is negative.
Here are some examples:

Positive statement	*Negative question tag*
It's a nice day,	isn't it?
You can understand me,	can't you?
He will help us,	won't he?
They must answer,	mustn't they?

If the statement is negative, the question tag is positive. Here are some examples:

Negative statement	*Positive question tag*
I haven't explained this,	have I?

You don't understand this,	do you?
She wasn't asked,	was she?
She needn't come,	need she?
You haven't broken the cup,	have you?
You daren't do that,	dare you?

If the verb in the statement is in the present tense (and is not one of the 'peculiars') we use *do* (*does*), *don't* (*doesn't*) in the question tag.

Positive statement	*Negative question tag*
They know us,	don't they?
We know them,	don't we?
You understand that,	don't you?
He understands it,	doesn't he?
She speaks French,	doesn't she?

Negative statement	*Positive question tag*
They don't know us,	do they?
We don't know them,	do we?
You don't understand that,	do you?
He doesn't understand it,	does he?

If the verb in the statement is in the past tense (and is not one of the 'peculiars') we use *did* (*didn't*) in the question tag. Examples:

Positive statement	*Negative question tag*
They knew us,	didn't they?
You understood that,	didn't you?
She spoke French,	didn't she?

Negative statement	*Positive question tag*
They didn't know us,	did they?
You didn't understand that,	did you?
She didn't speak French,	did she?

The only verbs that can be used in question tags are the 'peculiars'.

Meaning of tag questions

These questions in the form of **statement** plus **question tag** can have two quite different meanings.

1 If our voice rises on the question tag,

> He's English, isn't he?

we are really asking a question. We want to know. We think he's English, but we want an answer: *Yes, he is* or *No, he isn't*.

2 If our voice falls on the **question tag**,

> He's English, isn't he?

we just want the other person to agree with us. We are sure he's English. Probably we don't even wait for an answer.

JANE: If we meet **question tags** in writing – in a book or a letter – how do we know which meaning to understand?

TEACHER: From the *context*. You remember what that means, Karen, don't you?

KAREN: I think so. It means from the other sentences or the other words with it.

TEACHER: Yes. Look at this conversation from a book:

> A. 'It's a very ugly duckling.'
> B. 'Yes, it is ugly, isn't it?'
> A. 'Perhaps it isn't a duckling.'

What does the context tell you about B's remark?

BARBARA: He or she is just agreeing, not asking a real question.

TEACHER: Yes, the context tells you that. If you read it aloud, your voice would fall on the **question tag**. Here is another example:

> A. 'Is it a good film?'
> B. 'You've seen it, haven't you?'
> A. 'No. As a matter of fact I haven't.'

JANE: I understand now. That's a real question. B doesn't know the answer. His or her voice rises on the *haven't you*.

Exercises

A Add **question tags** to the following. Number 1 is done for you.

1 You haven't finished yet, *have you*?
2 He didn't answer.
3 We can come too.
4 I won't see you tomorrow.
5 He mustn't speak.
6 I don't know him.
7 They oughtn't to speak.
8 He answered.
9 He daren't ask us.
10 He must speak.
11 We can come too.
12 He didn't ask us.
13 I'll see you tomorrow.
14 They ought to speak.
15 I know him.
16 He doesn't understand what we say.
17 They won't stay away tomorrow.
18 We can't take animals to school.
19 We mustn't spend all this money.
20 You couldn't answer all the questions.
21 It hasn't rained for weeks.
22 There isn't enough for all of us.
23 There won't be enough for all of us.
24 There will be enough for all of us.
25 We won't have another lesson for a week.
26 Margaret sings better than Mary.
27 Mary doesn't sing as well as Margaret.
28 You've been here before.
29 You haven't been here before.
30 He never does what you tell him.
31 You didn't speak to him.

32 You spoke to him.
33 They sang a lot of songs.
34 They didn't sing many songs.
35 He writes to you often.
36 He wrote to you every day.
37 He didn't write to you every day.

B Try to put some of your answers in A into context, and speak them with the right fall or rise in your voice on the **question tag**.

Lesson Twenty-one

Short answers

Let's take another point about the 'peculiars'. Quite often
when we are asked a question, we give a 'short answer'; that
is, we leave out part of the answer. An example will show
what I mean. If you were asked the question, 'Do you go to
school every day?' your answer could be, 'Yes, I go to school
every day'. But you would be more likely to give the 'short
answer': 'Yes, I do'. Here are some more examples of the
full answer and the 'short answer'.

Question	Full answer	Short answer
Have you brought your book?	Yes, I have brought my book.	Yes, I have.
Did you understand the lesson?	Yes, I understood the lesson.	Yes, I did.
Can you swim?	Yes, I can swim.	Yes, I can.
Doesn't Richard like grammar?	No, he doesn't like grammar.	No, he doesn't.
Hasn't he finished the exercise?	No, he hasn't finished the exercise.	No, he hasn't.
Will the teacher be pleased?	No, he won't be pleased.	No, he won't.
Dare he climb that tree?	No, he daren't climb that tree.	No, he daren't.

And look at the verbs in the 'short answers'. Do you notice
which they are?

There's another kind of short answer. The questions begin
with an **interrogative pronoun** (Book 3, Lesson 2).

Question: Who is the stronger, Mr Bingo or Mr Jingo?
Long answer: Mr Jingo is the stronger.
Short answer: Mr Jingo is.

Question: Who can do this exercise?
Long answer: I can do this exercise.
Short answer: I can.

Question: Who must try harder?
Long answer: Richard must try harder.
Short answer: Richard must.

Question: Who will get into trouble if he doesn't try harder?
Long answer: Richard will get into trouble if he doesn't try
             harder.
Short answer: Richard will.

With the present tense, for all verbs except the 'peculiars' we use *do, does, don't, doesn't* for short answers.

Question: Who speaks English?
Long answer: I speak English.
Short answer: I do.

Question: Who often comes to school late?
Long answer: Richard often comes to school late.
Short answer: Richard does.

Question: Who doesn't understand this?
Long answer: I don't understand this. *or* Richard doesn't
             understand this.
Short answer: I don't. *or* Richard doesn't.

With the past tense, for all verbs except the 'peculiars' we use *did, didn't*.

Question: Who wrote this?
Long answer: I wrote it. *or* John wrote it.
Short answer: I did. *or* John did.

Question: Who didn't finish the exercise?
Long answer: I (*or* Helen) didn't finish the exercise.
Short answer: I (*or* Helen) didn't.

Question: Who went to Trinidad last week?
Long answer: I (*or* Joyce) went to Trinidad last week.
Short answer: I (*or* Joyce) did.

Notice again the verbs in those short answers!

Sometimes short answers are used to express agreement or disagreement.

Statement	*Agreement*
John is working well.	Yes, he is.
Lance has a lot of money.	Yes, he has.
It was a lovely day yesterday.	Yes, it was.
You've dropped your handkerchief.	So I have!
You said that before.	So I did!

Statement	*Disagreement*
Richard is working well.	No, he isn't.
It will take a long time to do that.	No, it won't.
This book costs a lot of money.	No, it doesn't.
You said that before.	No, I didn't.
Why didn't you say you knew him?	But I did.
You're always late for your lesson.	Oh no, I'm not.

And once again the verbs in the short answers are our little friends *be, have, can, do,* etc.

The only verbs you can use in short answers are the 'peculiars'.

Exercises

A Give first the full answer and then the 'short answer' (beginning 'Yes') to the following questions:

1 Have you read this book?
2 Can you speak English?
3 Will you come for a walk?
4 Have you met my Uncle Arthur?
5 Are you boys playing football?
6 Must I be there at 4 o'clock?
7 Does Richard like cakes?
8 Were you at the party last night?
9 Is that boy with the brown hair John?
10 Did you hear what he said?
11 Will you be fourteen tomorrow?

B Give first the full answer and then the short answer (beginning 'No') to the following questions:

1 Have you spoken to him?
2 Can you swim across the river?
3 Have you been to Trinidad?
4 Are the girls playing in the field?
5 Does Richard always give the right answers?
6 Did Richard give the right answer yesterday?
7 Did the boys climb the tree?
8 Must I be there at four o'clock? (See Lesson 16)
9 Will you be fourteen tomorrow?

C Give first the full answer, then the short answer, to each of the following questions:

1 Who is the better swimmer, Karen or Mary?
2 Who can open this door?
3 Who will help me to move this table?
4 Who did that exercise correctly?

5 Who didn't do the exercise correctly?
6 Who gets up every morning at seven o'clock? (Give two
answers, (1) beginning 'I . . .', and (2) beginning
'John . . .')

D Agree with the following (use short answers):

1 It's raining hard now. Yes . . .
2 But it was worse yesterday. Yes . . .
3 That window is open. So . . .
4 Your Uncle Arthur gave you that bicycle. Yes . . .
5 I told you the answer yesterday. So . . .
6 There's a mouse eating that apple. So . . .
7 We'll see what happens when the cat comes this way.
Yes . . .

E Disagree with the following:

1 It isn't raining now. No . . .
2 This train stops at Greenfields station. No . . .
3 It stopped there yesterday. No . . .
4 Why didn't you tell me so? But . . .
5 John likes to stay up late at night. Oh no, . . .
6 Joyce has plenty of money. Oh no, . . .
7 Why are you angry with me? But . . .

Lesson Twenty-two

The 'peculiars':
additions to remarks

There is another fairly common construction in which we make an addition to a remark. Here's an example of what I mean:

Remark	*Addition*
Margaret can play the piano,	and so *can I*.
We have a good teacher,	and so *have you*.
Richard ought to work harder,	and so *ought Joan*.
Our class will have a holiday tomorrow,	and so *will yours*.

Notice that when we make the addition there is **inversion** of the verb and subject: *can I* (not *I can*); *have you* (not *you have*); *ought Joan* (not *Joan ought*).

With the **present tense** of all **verbs** except the 'peculiars' we use *do* (*does*).

John cycles to school every morning, *and so do I*.
I cycle to school every morning, *and so does John*.

With the **past tense** of all **verbs** except the 'peculiars' we use *did*.

Richard scored a goal, *and so did Tom*.
Mary came to school early, *and so did I*.

There is a negative form of this construction. In that case we use *neither* or *nor*, again with **inversion** of the **subject** and **verb**. Here are some examples:

Mary can't play the piano, *neither (nor) can Jane*.
We haven't got a good teacher, *neither (nor) have you*.

Lesson Twenty-two

Our class won't have a holiday tomorrow, *neither will yours.*
Mary doesn't play the piano, *neither does Jane.*
John didn't score a goal, *neither did James.*

Notice that the remark is **negative,** but there is **affirmative** in the addition: *can* (not *can't*), *have* (not *haven't*), *will* (not *won't*).

I don't think I need tell you which are the only verbs that can be used in 'additions'!

Just one final point before we leave the 'peculiars'. The usual position for such adverbs as *generally, never, always, sometimes, nearly, often*, etc., is before the **verb.**

I *always* sleep with my windows open.
Richard *never* gets his exercises right.
We *often* cycle to school.
I *nearly* missed the train.
Mary *sometimes* cooks the dinner.

But with some **verbs** they go after the verb. Can you guess which ones? Here are some examples:

I have *never* seen him.
He is *always* busy when I call.
Richard can *always* find time for a game of football.
He may *sometimes* make a mistake; he doesn't *often* make one.
You needn't *always* do every exercise.

The usual place for the adverbs *generally, never, always, sometimes, nearly, often*, etc., is after the 'peculiars'.

Exercises

A Add 'additions' to these remarks. Don't forget the **inversion**. (The **subject** of the addition is given in brackets.)

1 Richard can't sing. (John)
2 Mary wasn't late for school. (Elizabeth)
3 Helen hasn't brought any food. (William)
4 That cap isn't mine. (this)
5 Those books aren't mine. (these)
6 He oughtn't to say such things. (you)
7 We didn't know the right time. (they)
8 Mary doesn't stay up late at night. (Joanna)
9 Richard won't be fourteen tomorrow. (Edward)
10 Mary won't be fourteen tomorrow. (I)

B Rewrite the following sentences putting the **adverbs** (in brackets) in the correct position.

1 I get up at seven o'clock (always).
2 He has done this before (never).
3 Lloyd and George are early for school (generally). Richard comes late (usually).
4 Mary comes to our house (often). Margaret has come with her (sometimes).
5 I think (sometimes) that Richard will learn grammar (never).
6 We have finished our work (nearly); I forgot (nearly) it had to be done by six o'clock.
7 It isn't easy (always) to do something that you have done before (never).
8 I have seen a fox in these woods (never) but my father says he saw one (often) when he was a boy.
9 We go for a holiday (sometimes) in May and we get good weather (usually).
10 We go for a holiday in August (generally) and we have had good weather (nearly always). (Remember *had* is sometimes a full verb. See Lesson 18.)

WHICH ARE THE ONLY VERBS THAT

HAVE CONTRACTED FORMS ?

MAKE THEIR INTERROGATIVES BY INVERSION ?

ARE USED FOR SHORT ANSWERS ?

MAKE THE EMPHATIC FORM ?

ARE USED FOR QUESTION TAGS ?

MAKE THEIR NEGATIVE BY ADDING 'NOT' OR 'N'T' ONLY ?

ARE AUXILIARIES ?

TAKE ADVERBS LIKE ALWAYS, SOMETIMES, OFTEN, NEARLY, ETC. AFTER THEM ?

ARE USED FOR ADDITIONS TO REMARKS ?

MAY HAVE DO SHOULD

MUST BE CAN NEED

DARE OUGHT TO

USED TO WILL

WE ARE !!

A word or two on punctuation

The aim of punctuation is to make the meaning of a passage more clearly and easily understood. A complete difference of meaning can be caused by a difference of punctuation. Look at these two sentences, for example. The words in each are exactly the same; it is the punctuation that makes the difference.

1 Richard said, 'The teacher is silly.'
2 'Richard,' said the teacher, 'is silly.'

And there is an old story about a barber who put up a notice:

> What do you think
> I shave you for nothing
> and give you a drink

Customers came to his shop expecting a free shave and a free drink. But he explained that the notice should be read like this:

> What! Do you think I shave
> you for nothing and give you a drink?

Many of the most commonly used punctuation marks are illustrated in the examples given above. These are quotation marks or inverted commas (' . . . '), used to show **direct speech** (Book 3, Lesson 21); the exclamation mark (!), used after an **interjection** (Book 1, Lesson 20) or expression of strong feeling; the question mark (?), used after a **direct question** (Book 4, Lesson 6), but not after an **indirect question**; the comma (,) and the full stop (.).

The full stop, the colon (:), the semicolon (;) and the comma

are generally used to show the pause that you would make in
speaking the words. The full stop marks the longest pause;
the comma, the shortest pause; the semicolon marks a longer
pause than the comma.

The full stop is used:
1 At the end of all sentences except questions and
exclamations.
   He needs your help. (statement)
   Help him. (command)
   Will you help him? (question)
   He cried, 'Help! Help!' (exclamation)
2 After abbreviations such as M.A. (= Master of Arts),
H.M.S. *Valiant* (= Her Majesty's ship *Valiant*), U.S.A. (=
United States of America), e.g. (= exempli gratia (*Latin*) =
for example), etc. Sometimes we miss out the full stops in
such abbreviations: USA, USSR.

The colon is used:
1 To separate sentences when the second explains more fully
the meaning of the first. It often means the same as 'that is to
say'.
   Richard's work is unsatisfactory: his answers are
   thoughtless, his spelling is careless, and his writing is bad.
2 To introduce a number of items in a list.
   Some commonly used punctuation marks are: full stop,
   colon, and comma.

The semicolon is useful when we need a longer pause than is
indicated by a comma, but when we don't want to break the
line of thought, as would happen if we used a full stop. You
will find more semicolons in old-fashioned writing than in
modern reading matter.

The comma is the most frequently used punctuation mark
and has many uses. Your common sense and the desire to
make your meaning clear will often tell you where you want

to make a pause, but these 'rules', though they don't cover all the uses, may be helpful.

A comma is generally used:

1 To record a list of objects, etc.

   At the party we had cakes, jellies, ices, biscuits, chocolate and lemonade.

Notice that the comma is not usually put before *and* and the last item.

2 To mark off direct speech.

   'Tell me,' he said, 'how you know all that.'

   The trapper replied, 'I heard it on the radio.'

3 To mark off sentences or clauses where a pause is needed in reading. This is almost always the case when an **adverb clause** comes before the **main clause**.

   Although it was foggy, we played the match.

   I have explained this work to Richard, but he still doesn't understand it.

   If you will help me, I will help you.

4 To mark off words used in addressing a person.

   George, tell Richard the answer to the question.

   I hope, sir, my answer is right.

5 To mark off words or phrases like *however, therefore, of course, for instance,* etc.

   You know, of course, what a gerund is; I needn't, therefore, explain it now.

6 In **apposition** (Lesson 12).

   Elizabeth II, Queen of Great Britain, was born in 1926.

   I saw Mr Shah, your teacher, this morning.

7 To mark off phrases containing a **participle** when a pause is required in reading.

   Seeing that his brother was hurt, George ran to help him.

   Remembering how fond you are of fruit, I've brought you some apples from our garden.

8 To separate off a **non-restrictive adjective clause** (Lesson 1).

   Jane was on her old bicycle, which was bright red.

9 To separate a **tag question** from the **statement** it follows.
   She speaks French, doesn't she?

Exercises

A Rewrite this little story, and put in the punctuation.
Include capital letters where they are needed.

the following was written on the gravestone of an army mule
here lies maggie the mule who in her time kicked a general
two colonels four majors ten captains twenty-four lieutenants
forty sergeants two hundred and twenty privates and a bomb

B Do the same with this story, and put in an apostrophe (')
where it is needed.

i cant understand it said mr williams oh what cant you
understand said his friend well said mr williams just look at
this suit im wearing the wool was grown in australia the cloth
was woven in yorkshire the buttons were made in india the
suit was made in london and i bought it in cairo whats so
remarkable about that asked his friend isnt it wonderful said
mr williams taking no notice of the interruption that so many
people can make a living out of something i havent paid for

C Do the same with this story. You will need exclamation
marks (!).

a very agitated woman rang up her doctor and an assistant
answered the phone can i speak to dr russell she said its
urgent im sorry madam the doctor is out will you leave a
message oh dear oh dear my ten year old little boy has
swallowed a fountain pen when will the doctor be in im afraid
madam he wont be in for two hours perhaps three hours
three hours cried the woman what shall i do in the meantime
im afraid madam youll have to use a pencil

GOODBYE

Well, that's the end of *Brighter Grammar*. You've now had a general outline, a 'bird's-eye view' of English Grammar, and you've met some of the chief 'rules'. (They have been printed in heavy type so that you will remember them.) Just a word about those 'rules' so that you don't get any wrong ideas. We don't want you to get a picture in your mind of an old grammarian, hundreds of years ago, saying to a very young English Language (just as a schoolmaster might speak to a rather disobedient little boy): 'So you are the English Language, are you? Well, my boy, here's a list of rules that I have made, and you must obey them!'

That's quite a wrong picture. The English Language came long before the grammarian. Grammarians are merely people who have observed the language at work and have said, 'So far as we can see, this is how the English Language works. We've studied it at work and we've written down what we have observed. Sometimes it behaves like other languages, like Latin or French or German, for example. Sometimes (you remember the 'peculiars') it behaves quite differently from other languages.' Their attitude is like Newton discovering the law of gravity or modern scientists studying the atom. These scientists don't say, 'Look, Nature, here are some laws that you must obey.' Scientists don't work like that. They say rather, 'We have studied nature and tried to discover its working, and this is what we have discovered. These, so far as we can see at present, are the laws of nature.'

Lesson Twenty-three

In *Brighter Grammar* we have tried to approach grammar in the same 'scientific' way. In these books you have seen us and the students (even Richard!) trying to see how the language works and to tell you what we discover. We have tried to show you that English Grammar is not a collection of dull, dead words but a living thing. It is a living tree, slowly but constantly growing and changing; not a dead, decaying log. Some of its limbs may gradually die and fall away (the old use of *shall* is one of them), but new life springs out at the tips of its branches; new words, new constructions take the place of those that die.

And when you see grammar in this light, then we believe that 'dreary grammar' becomes 'brighter grammar'.

C.E. ECKERSLEY
MARGARET MACAULAY